WE BECOME A POEM

NOS VOLVEMOS POEMA

A bilingual collection of poems without translation

Una colección de poemas bilingüe sin traducción

Silvi Galmozzi

Language Acquisition Books

Sinagazi
PUBLISHING

Published by Sinagazi LLC
www.sinagazi.com
contact@sinagazi.com

ISBN: 978-1-968514-04-4

Cover and interior design by Sinagazi LLC
Printed in the United States of America

First Edition: 2025

Dedication / Dedicatoria

To everyone who speaks in two voices, feels with two hearts, and calls more than one place home.

A quienes hablan con dos voces, sienten con dos corazones, y llaman hogar a más de un lugar.

Acknowledgments / Agradecimientos

Thank you to every teacher, friend, stranger, ancestor, and poet who gave me a word, a rhythm, or a silence that stayed with me. Your languages live in mine.

Gracias a cada maestra, amigo, desconocido, ancestro y poeta que me regaló una palabra, un ritmo o un silencio que se quedó conmigo. Sus lenguas viven en la mía.

Author's Note / Nota de la autora

I was raised by the Argentine sun, and reshaped by the rain of the Pacific Northwest. I've lived long enough between languages to know they're not just tools—they're textures. They hold memory, identity, history, joy, contradiction. Sometimes, I feel like I'm not two people, but one soul stretched across two sound systems.

Fui criada por el sol argentino, y transformada por la lluvia del noroeste del Pacífico. He vivido lo suficiente entre idiomas como para saber que no son solo herramientas—son texturas. Llevan memoria, identidad, historia, alegría, contradicción. A veces siento que no soy dos personas, sino un alma extendida entre dos sistemas de sonido.

This book is not translated. It's lived, in two voices. It is a home for those of us who exist in the in-between—with love, without apology.

Este libro no está traducido. Está vivido, en dos voces. Es un hogar para quienes existimos en el intermedio—con amor, sin disculpas.

Introduction / Introducción

I was born in Argentina—where Spanish is not just a language, but a dance, a melody, a way of feeling. I now live in the United States, where English is part of my everyday life: my career, my friendships, my routines. Two homes. Two identities. Two languages—that are, in truth, one body with two hearts.

Nací en Argentina—donde el español no es solo un idioma, sino una danza, una melodía, una forma de sentir. Hoy vivo en Estados Unidos, donde el inglés forma parte de mi vida diaria: mi trabajo, mis amistades, mis rutinas. Dos hogares. Dos identidades. Dos idiomas—que en realidad son un solo cuerpo con dos corazones.

This book is not a language manual. It is not a translation workbook. It is a collection of poems born from the space between languages—what we call macaronic, where Spanish and English live together, line by line, sentence by sentence. No translations. Just coexistence. Just breath.

Este libro no es un manual de idiomas. No es un cuaderno de traducciones. Es una colección de poemas nacidos del espacio entre lenguas—lo que llamamos macarrónico, donde el español y el inglés conviven, línea por línea, frase por frase. Sin traducciones. Solo coexistencia. Solo respiración.

What to Expect / Qué esperar

We Become a Poem is a bilingual journey through identity, language, and cultural connection, written in both English and Spanish. Rather than offering side-by-side translations, each poem exists as its own piece—sometimes flowing between languages within a single line, other times exploring one language fully before shifting to the other. The book is divided into thematic sections that reflect personal and shared experiences: from intimate reflections on belonging to universal moments of travel, language, and human connection. You'll find poems that celebrate cultural heritage, honor linguistic evolution, and reflect on the historical weight of colonization and migration. This book is for anyone who lives between worlds, speaks between languages, or finds themselves in the poetry of in-between spaces.

Nos volvemos poema es un viaje bilingüe a través de la identidad, el lenguaje y la conexión cultural, escrito en inglés y en español. En lugar de ofrecer traducciones paralelas, cada poema existe por sí mismo: a veces fluye entre idiomas dentro de un solo verso, otras veces explora uno completamente antes de cambiar al otro. El libro está dividido en secciones temáticas que reflejan experiencias tanto personales como universales: desde reflexiones íntimas sobre el sentido de pertenencia hasta momentos compartidos de viaje, lenguaje y conexión humana. Encontrarás poemas que celebran la herencia cultural, honran la evolución lingüística y reflexionan sobre el peso histórico de la colonización y la migración. Este libro es para quienes viven entre mundos, hablan entre idiomas o se reconocen en la poesía de los espacios intermedios.

Table of Contents / Tabla de contenidos

A reverent closing section exploring race, class, ancestry, migration, and the profound impact history has on language and identity.

Una sección final reverente que explora la raza, la clase, la herencia, la migración y el profundo impacto de la historia en el idioma y la identidad.

Between Us / Entre Nosotras

No quiero quererte

No quiero quererte,
I just can't help it,
En tu mirada veo
my soul's reflection,
like a verse I never wrote
but always knew.
Te pienso en inglés,
I dream of you in Spanish,
and somewhere in between
we become a poem.
Te busco en las palabras,
the ones that rhyme with stay,
pero el idioma del alma
no se puede traducir, anyway.

Tiempo sin reloj

El tiempo no avisa,
it passes in the blink of un recuerdo.
La juventud cree que siempre
habrá más summers, más intentos,
más chances to say te quiero without fear.
I wore my youth like a borrowed jacket,
too big for my shoulders,
con bolsillos llenos de sueños
and a tear near the heart
donde el amor se escapaba.
Sabiduría llegó en susurros,
not in textbooks,
but in noches sin dormir,
cuando la piel ya no brilla
pero el alma aprende a hablar.
La vejez no es castigo,
it's a second childhood,
donde las arrugas cuentan cuentos
y el silencio tiene acento.
Es cuando finally, entiendes.
And still, el tiempo sigue,
measuring nothing
but how brave you were
entre el primer suspiro
y el último adiós.

Where I Come From

I come from calles that whisper,
de esquinas que conocen mi nombre,
from madres who say bendición
even when their hands are empty
and their hearts, full.
There, el viento huele a historias,
a pan casero y promesas rotas,
and even the silence
speaks with an accent
que no se olvida.
I carry it all—the prayers, the palmas,
the fights en la cocina,
my abuela's laughter
floating like incense at dusk.
No soy de aquí, ni de allá,
I walk between, barefoot,
with dust on my tongue
and two languages
braided into my breath.
Where I come from
is not a map,
es una canción sin final,
the kind you hum
cuando no sabes volver.

Half-Translated

I live between languages,
conjugating myself daily
en una tierra que me llama foreigner
aunque llevo su clima en mi piel
y its rhythm in my bones.
Back home, if I can still call it that,

soy turista de mi propia niñez,
asking for directions
en la lengua de mi madre,
but with doubt in the accent.
I shop with a smile,
pero hago cuentas en español.
I laugh in English,
pero cuando lloro,
the tears whisper 'ay, mija'.
The passport says citizen.
The tongue says exile.
The mirror reflects alguien
que nunca quite belongs,
but still blooms.
And so I write,
poemas that stretch across borders,
sewn with palabras that resist translation,
hoping someday to be understood
just as I am—sin subtítulos.

She Was Told

She was told
to speak clearly,
que no mezclara idiomas
porque the world prefers
its boxes tidy.
Her name was shortened,
rounded, softened—un acento eliminado
como si fuera error
instead of herencia.
It was said
she'd forget where she came from
if she stayed too long
where roots don't hold,
where seasons don't sing her lullabies.
Yet at night,
cuando nadie miraba,
she whispered both languages
into the same prayer,
and they answered.

She Was Given

She was given
two tongues to taste the world,
dos formas de decir te amo,
and twice as many chances
to listen with her soul.
At first, it felt like too much,
demasiadas palabras,
not enough space.
But soon, each lengua
became a bridge.
She was handed
music from both sides,
villancicos y lullabies,
and in every note,
she heard belonging.
Even when accents tangled,
cuando las frases se mezclaban,
what mattered was connection,
and she carried that
in every conversation.

They Say

They say
she was lucky,
tener dos mundos
to call her own.
And they were right.
She could taste culture
like a recipe passed down
con instrucciones en Spanglish,
and every dish
told a story she understood.
At work,
her words translated bridges,
not just idioms but intención.
At home,
she dreamt in colors unnamed.
They say
some things get lost
in translation.
But she knew—some things are only found there.

A Life Woven

Her life was woven
entre sílabas y calles,
between how are you?
and ¿cómo amaneciste?
in threads no map could trace.
Stories found her
in cafés and mercados,
in English smiles
and Spanish nods.
She belonged in every gesture.
Love letters came
in mismatched grammar,
but perfect meaning.
The kind that says:
You see me. In both languages.
No single country held her.
Ningún idioma la limitó.
She became the translation
of herself—whole, hybrid, home.

Where We Meet / Donde Coincidimos

Borderless

A plate is passed,
una historia is shared,
and suddenly,
no one's foreign.
Language becomes a bridge,
not a test.
Accents?
A kind of music
con su propio compás.
Where there is food,
hay memoria.
Where there is dance,
hay diálogo.
And if you listen,
really listen,
even silence
tells you where it's from.

Tierra Ajena, Tierra Mía

Una calle ajena
smells like pan recién hecho.
Someone laughs
in a rhythm you don't know—yet you smile anyway.
The signs
are in a language
you once feared,
but now they read
like poetry in disguise.
Foreignness fades
en la curiosidad,
in the trying,
in the nods of waiters
when you say gracias
with a tourist tongue.

Soundtrack of Elsewhere

It starts with a beat,
el pulso de otra tierra.
Maybe it's salsa, maybe soul,
maybe something you've never heard
but somehow remember.
Music doesn't ask for papers.
It lets you in
if your body says yes.
A chorus in another tongue
can still break your heart,
or fix it.
And the chorus repeats
otra vez, otra vez
until it feels
like home.

La Lengua del Mercado

No one needs subtitles
in the mercado.
A hand gesture,
a smile,
el olor de mango maduro.
Here, commerce is culture.
Bargaining is poetry.
And every voice
gritty, melodic, rushed
adds to the song.
Languages braid themselves
over the produce.
Dollars, pesos, dirhams,
all spoken in the same hope:
Que te vaya bien.

Flavor Memory

The first bite
tastes like someone else's childhood.
Una sopa con nombres nuevos,
but something in the warmth
feels known.
Spices speak
in syllables you don't understand,
but your body listens anyway.
El paladar no miente:
it remembers everything.
Recipes cross oceans.
No visa required.
And somewhere in the chewing
you realize—you've been welcomed.

Una Niñez Prestada

A borrowed childhood
lives in the plaza,
where voices rise like birds
y los juegos no necesitan traducción.
Marbles, rainwater,
el sonido de tambores lejanos
even if it wasn't yours,
it still feels yours
cuando cierras los ojos.
Kids don't ask,
Where are you from?
They ask,
Quieres jugar?
And just like that,
you belong.

Mixed Plate

A little bit of curry,
a little bit of chorizo,
tortillas meet turmeric
on the same dish—and no one fights.
Fusion is not confusion.
Es evolución.
The table grows
with every guest
que trae algo nuevo.
And if you let your palate lead,
you'll taste centuries
crisscrossed, spiced,
served on porcelain or palm leaves
but always offered
with both hands.

Footnotes

Every translation
is a kind of poem.
Not exact—nunca exacto
but faithful
to feeling.
Words stretch,
se doblan como cuerpos cansados
trying to say the unsayable.
The meaning lives
in the margin,
like a footnote
only the heart can read.
And so we speak,
not to be perfect,
but to be understood
en cualquier idioma
that will have us.

Cultures in Contrast / Culturas en Contraste

Small Talk, Big Distance

In some places,
How are you?
is just noise.
Un puente cortito
de cortesía vacía.
But elsewhere
¿Cómo amaneciste?
How did you sleep?
comes with mate,
con pan,
with time.
English says "I'm fine"
cuando el corazón
is breaking quietly.
Spanish lingers,
sits with you,
no se va tan rápido.
And still,
in both languages,
we learn to hear
what wasn't said.

Cortesmente Polite

They say in Scotland,
sarcasm is affection.
In México,
the diminutivo
makes everything tender
cafecito, abracito, amorcito.
Australia greets you
with a grin and a nickname.
Colombia with an hola preciosa
even if it's just the postman.
Each place teaches
its own version of kindness.
A hug,
a joke,
una palabra suave.
There is no single way
to mean welcome,
pero cuando se siente,
you know.

Clock People, Island Time

At 8:00 sharp,
ya es tarde
in Germany.
In Peru,
el tiempo es más elástico,
like the light at golden hour
soft and forgiving.
Americans schedule coffee.
Argentines live at cafés.
The English queue.
Los cubanos float.
Time
is cultural.
But connection
is always ahora.

Accent Is a Map

You can hear la tierra
in the way someone says water.
A Glaswegian twist,
un acento costeño,
a Texan drawl
stretched like summer heat.
Accents carry roots.
Marcan el ritmo
of stories,
of lullabies
sung just a little off-key
but perfectly.
"No' bother, mate."
"¡De una!"
"Cheers, love."
"¿Qué más pues?"
None of them mean exactly
what they say,
but all of them say:
I'm from somewhere. I bring it with me.

Bailar Is a Verb for Living

To dance is to speak
without needing permission.
En Cuba, hips know
what drums want.
In England, feet tap shyly
but sincerely.
An Argentine tango
tells a full novela
in one slow ochenta.
A Texan two-step
says hello with a twirl
and thank you with a stomp.
And when no one's watching,
hasta los tímidos
bailan a escondidas.
Because somewhere inside,
todos llevamos
una canción.

Dicho, Then Done

Cada país tiene
su propio oráculo
a way to say
what can't be taught.
In Puerto Rico:
Más vale tarde que con hambre.
In Ireland:
What's the craic?
In Chile:
Más chileno que los porotos.
In the South of the U.S.:
Bless your heart
(could mean anything.)
They're not just sayings
son mapas del alma.
A proverb,
a shrug,
a wink disguised as wisdom.
Language may change,
pero los dichos
se heredan.

The Door Was Open

Some cultures knock.
Others walk right in,
con un beso, un saludo,
and a ¿comiste?
In Guatemala,
a stranger gets coffee
before they get questions.
In Texas,
make yourself at home
isn't a suggestion—it's the law.
There are homes
where shoes are removed,
where prayers are whispered,
where the smell of sopa
meets you like a hug.
And even when you're far from home,
una mesa puesta,
a warm seat offered,
makes you remember
you're not alone.

Sacred Is a Common Word

They call it luck.
They call it fate.
Lo llaman destino,
o Dios,
o la energía del universo.
In New Zealand, the land is alive.
En Perú, las montañas escuchan.
In the American South,
every storm is a sermon.
In Spain, the cathedral breathes.
People light candles.
Otros riegan agua bendita.
Someone lays a crystal
next to their grandmother's photo
and prays for peace
en dos idiomas.
No matter the name,
what is sacred
is felt.
And sometimes,
that's all it needs to be.

Fiesta Is a Verb

In some places,
celebration is loud
una cumbia que no termina,
fireworks,
la tía dancing barefoot
con una copa en la mano.
Elsewhere,
it's quiet
a pint with friends,
una sonrisa sincera,
un brindis discreto.
Laughter sounds different
in every country,
but joy?
It's unmistakable.
Una carcajada is a passport.
Even grief gets music,
porque en esta vida,
we dance with it all
the sorrow,
the healing,
the punchline at the end.

Languages with History / Lenguas con Historia

The Tree of Tongues

All languages
were once one whisper,
una raíz profunda
beneath the soil of time.
From there,
the words branched out
leaves of amor and love,
night and noche,
shaped by wind, by war,
by who stayed
and who wandered.
Some branches withered.
Others grew thorns.
But still they reached,
speaking in new directions.
Language is not born
it grows.

Colonial Echoes

They came with ships,
cruces y coronas,
and tongues sharp enough
to carve borders
in the air.
Spanish spread
like a prayer and a sword.
English followed
with laws and ledgers.
But even in conquest,
la lengua se mezcló.
In markets, in marriages,
en canciones cantadas en secreto.
What they tried to erase,
bloomed back
in accents,
in rhythms,
en palabras que se resistieron a morir.

Borrowed Words

We don't say it often,
but English is a thief
plaza, patio, fiesta,
tucked into its pockets
like travel souvenirs.
And Spanish?
It cradles its own borrowings
té, fútbol, whisky
spoken with sabor nuevo.
Languages don't steal
they seduce.
They flirt with sound.
They marry meaning.
And we are the children
of their unions.

The Mouth Remembers

Even if the mind forgets,
la boca recuerda.
It curls the r
like it did en la infancia.
It slows for th,
tiptoes around v and b,
stumbles through squirrel
like it's carrying stones.
Accent is memory.
It is lineage in the lips,
ancestry between syllables.
Every word we say
carries footprints
of those who spoke before us.

Desde el Latín, Con Amor

Las palabras vienen del latín,
desnudas, suaves,
listas para vestirse
con acentos nuevos.
Mater se hizo madre,
frater se volvió hermano,
y el amor,
ese no cambió tanto.
Del latín al romance,
de la península
al continente,
de monasterios a mercados
el idioma caminó.
Y aún hoy,
cuando dices amor,
la raíz responde:
te estaba esperando.

Las Lenguas que se Van

Algunas lenguas
se están muriendo en silencio.
Sin ceremonias.
Sin adiós.
Ya no se escucha el zapoteco
en la plaza.
El ainu duerme
en la garganta de los abuelos.
El taíno aún canta,
pero muy bajito.
Se pierden
porque no se escribieron,
porque no se escuchan
en las noticias,
porque no vendían.
Pero si cierras los ojos,
y dices su nombre,
la lengua despierta
solo un poco.
Solo para ti.

Gramática Es un Fantasma

La gramática no se ve,
pero vive en nosotros.
Nos dice cuándo callar,
cuándo preguntar,
cuándo decir lo siento
aunque no lo estemos.
It's the ghost in the sentence,
el eco en la estructura.
Una fuerza invisible
que da forma a lo que pensamos
sin que lo sepamos.
Porque decir yo fui
no es lo mismo que yo iba.
Y eso lo sabe el alma,
aunque no recuerdes por qué.

Sueños Criollos

Entre los colonizadores
y los esclavizados,
nacieron lenguas nuevas.
Lenguas híbridas.
Lenguas valientes.
Papiamento,
palabras africanas bailando con el español.
Haitian Creole,
con el ritmo del francés y la resistencia.
Jamaican Patois,
English twisted,
jubiloso,
rebeldía con flow.
Estas lenguas no piden permiso.
Son hijas del caos y del cariño.
Y su existencia
es una victoria.

El Idioma del Futuro

Las palabras del futuro
may not be spelled the way we think.
Quizás mezclen inglés, español y memes,
spoken through apps, en tiempo real.
Dirán lol, qué risa,
they'll say bro and compa with the same breath.
Las generaciones que vienen
won't ask permission to blend.
Grammar will stretch,
las reglas serán sugerencias.
Y aún así,
we'll understand each other just fine.
Porque el idioma del futuro
será el del corazón abierto.
And it will sound
like everyone,
and no one.
Al mismo tiempo.

¿Por Qué Hablamos?

Hablamos para no estar solos.
We speak to feel seen.
Decimos te quiero aunque duela,
we whisper I'm sorry when we're brave.
Llenamos silencios con palabras,
we fill pages so we won't forget.
A veces mentimos con la boca,
but the eyes always tell the truth.
El lenguaje no es perfecto,
but it's all we've got.
Y cuando no hay palabras suficientes,
we still try.
Porque hablar
es humano.
Y escuchar,
es amar.

We Carry the Words / Cargamos las Palabras

Rostros del Idioma

No hay un solo rostro
para el español.
No hay una piel oficial
para el inglés.
In México,
la lengua may sound light
en el norte,
y más lenta
cuando llega al sur.
In the U.S.,
your accent can betray
your zip code,
or your parents' struggle.
El idioma se lleva en la espalda,
en los dientes,
en el cuerpo que camina
con una historia.
Y aún así,
it belongs to all of us.

Lenguas Heredadas

They were not meant
to speak the master's tongue,
pero lo aprendieron
a golpes y canciones.
Los esclavos
cantaban en códigos,
susurros que bailaban
con el inglés que no pedían.
Indigenous words
se quedaron atrapadas
entre la cruz y la corona,
pero algunas escaparon
en la selva de la voz.
Now we say okay and canoa,
banana and bruja,
and carry in each syllable
a memory
of what was taken
and what survived.

El Precio del Habla

To speak properly
costs money.
Un acento "neutral"
se paga caro,
in tutors,
en silencio,
en corregirse mil veces.
In barrios,
se habla con sabor y calle.
In boardrooms,
se habla con filtros y miedo.
But neither is more true.
Because even slang
es resistencia,
and even formality
is a mask we wear
to be heard.

Palabras en la Maleta

They crossed borders
con una maleta,
una foto,
y un idioma a medias.
Children forgot
lo que los abuelos decían,
too busy learning how to fit in
sin acento,
sin error.
Pero a veces,
la lengua regresa
en sueños,
en canciones,
en el olor del arroz.
Language is never fully lost.
Se esconde.
Espera.
Then returns
when someone dares to open
la maleta de la memoria.

Survival Speech

They taught us
to speak well
pero callar mejor.
In English,
we learned to soften,
to smile with our vowels.
En español,
a bajarle dos rayitas,
a no sonar tan brava.
Code-switching
became instinct.
Un acto de defensa.
Un arte de sobrevivir.
We speak two languages
y también dos versiones
de nosotros mismos.
One to be safe.
Otra para ser real.

Neither, Ni

She looked white.
Hablaba español.
Y en inglés,
they asked,
Where are you really from?
Él nació en el Bronx
pero su abuela
era de las montañas.
He speaks in Spanglish,
con ritmo
y sin disculpas.
Neither fully this,
ni completamente aquello.
But maybe
what makes us whole
no es pertenecer,
sino mezclar—ser puente.
Ser eco.
Ser raíz múltiple.

La Voz es Poder

La voz temblaba,
pero no se cayó.
They said:
Speak louder.
But not like that.
Dijeron:
Eres muy emocional.
Muy fuerte.
Muy algo.
Pero la voz siguió
gritando en la plaza,
cantando en la cocina,
escribiendo en los márgenes.
Porque quien encuentra su voz,
encuentra el camino.
And once it's found,
no hay vuelta atrás.

Broken English, Español Roto

I speak like this,
she said,
but I understand everything.
Habla mocho,
le dijeron,
como si su boca fuera
una herramienta dañada.
But her words built bridges.
Las suyas,
levantaron techos de consuelo.
Perfection
is a myth.
Connection
es la verdadera fluidez.
Lo roto
también canta.

La Lengua de los Ancestros

Your tongue moves
con la memoria de otros.
It rolls its r,
bends its verbs,
con el ritmo
de quienes vinieron antes.
Tus abuelos tal vez no escribieron,
pero hablaban poesía
cuando decían mija,
cuando curaban con cuentos,
cuando llamaban al alma por su nombre.
Each word you say
has fingerprints.
Cada idioma que hablas
te habla también.

We Are Still Here, Aquí Seguimos

Despite it all
colonias, guerras,
castas, cadenas
here we are.
Aquí seguimos.
Speaking.
Singing.
Learning each other's names.
We carry pain,
sí.
But also:
cumbia, soul, laughter,
comida compartida,
lenguas revueltas
que no se rinden.
The world tried to divide us
by country, by color,
by class, by voice
but language said
we are not done.
Y no lo estamos.
Porque cada vez que hablamos
con el corazón abierto,
la historia se reescribe
en presente.

Final Reflection / Reflexión Final

Thank you for reading. Whether you read every word, skipped around, or let the rhythm of two languages carry you, I'm grateful you spent time here.

To live bilingually is to live with complexity, beauty, contradiction, and depth. It is a life filled with double meaning, double memory, and twice the ways to express who you are.

This book was written for those who navigate more than one culture, more than one language, and sometimes, more than one self. It's a celebration of that in-between space—not as a place of confusion, but as a place of creativity and connection.

Gracias por leer. Ya sea que hayas leído palabra por palabra, salteado páginas, o simplemente te hayas dejado llevar por el ritmo de los dos idiomas, gracias por estar aquí.

Vivir bilingüe es vivir con complejidad, con belleza, con contradicciones y profundidad. Es tener doble sentido, doble memoria, y más de una forma de expresar quién eres.

Este libro fue escrito para quienes habitan más de una cultura, más de un idioma, y a veces, más de un yo. Es una celebración de ese espacio intermedio—no con confusión, sino con creatividad y conexión.

Here's to the multilingual life.
Brindemos por la vida multilingüe.

With gratitude,
Con gratitud,
Silvi Galmozzi

About the Author

Silvi Galmozzi is a bilingual writer, language educator, and a pretty good car and shower dancer who believes in the power of language to build bridges. With roots in Argentina and a life shaped by travel, cultures, and good food, Silvi creates spaces where English and Spanish can dance together — with rhythm, honesty, and soul.

We Become a Poem is her first poetry collection.

You can find Silvi writing, dancing, and sipping Malbec in Oregon—always working on the next book.

About Sinagazi Publishing

Sinagazi LLC is an independent, bilingual publishing house dedicated to books that invite connection, curiosity, and courage. Sinagazi celebrates multilingual voices and seeks to create inclusive literary experiences rooted in language acquisition, accessibility, and cultural respect.

The tagline — **Read. Learn. Belong.** — is more than a slogan. It's an invitation.

Contact & Community

www.sinagazi.com

contact@sinagazi.com

www.ingramcontent.com/pod-product-compliance
Lightning Source LLC
Chambersburg PA
CBHW071525120626

46550CB00006B/2358